# LETTING GO

## Surrender, Release Attachments and Accept the Present

### B. L. HALLISON

ISBN: 1518810993
ISBN-13: 978-1518810992

# DEDICATED TO
# THE READER

May you discover peace,
harmony and happiness.

# TABLE OF CONTENTS

# INTRODUCTION

*The inward journey is about finding your own fullness, something that no one else can take away.*

–Deepak Chopra

We are all aware that we cling to negative thought patterns and habits. We obsess over how we look, even though deep down we know that judgments based on our appearances are shallow and meaningless. We stress over our responsibilities all of the time, even though life carries on whether we do the housework or not. We become unhappy if our relationships are not fruitful or if people around us do not celebrate or revere our presence.

Most other guides in the western world promise that if we can just improve ourselves, we can be happier. We just need to be a little more disciplined, a little fitter and a little smarter. It doesn't matter that we already seem exhausted and overwhelmed by the chaos and demands of modern life; others suggest we need to do more and be more.

This book, however, offers a different approach. The solution to all our stresses and anxieties and the key to true happiness is letting go of all our needless attachments. If we let go of our need to be beautiful, we do not let that stubborn facial acne or that dry skin ruin our day. If we let go of the desire for everyone to like us, we do not become frustrated when people do not. If we let go of the need for the house to be spotless, we can focus on what genuinely matters in our lives. We don't have to become careless about our appearance, let our houses become a mess or be rude to others - but we don't need to let these aspects of our lives cause ourselves suffering either. We just need to be.

The teachings discussed here will give you the knowledge and understanding needed to start letting go of all your harmful attachments. We will begin by first discussing the reasons and importance of *why* you need to let go of pointless and harmful attachments, by delving into a little Buddhist philosophy and eastern thought. In the second chapter, you will read and understand about *how* you can start to let go and live a happier life. Finally, in the last four chapters of this book you will be given practical and down-to-earth advice about small changes you can make to your life to be happier and let go of your attachments, informed by your new understanding of 'letting go'.

Thank you again for reading. You have already taken the first step towards letting go and living a more fulfilled life. I trust you will greatly benefit from its teachings.

# 1

## WHY SHOULD YOU 'LET GO'?

*You will find that it is necessary to let things go; simply for the reason that they are heavy. So let them go, let go of them. I tie no weights to my ankles.*

—C. JoyBell

Most of us would have heard about 'letting go' of our attachments at some point in our lives. Even if we don't know enough about the eastern philosophies from where this advice originates, many of us see the wisdom in letting things go. We all tend to be aware that we have habits that cause us pain; negative thinking patterns and unhelpful desires and attachments that may cause us to fret over the future or feel shameful about the past.

However, almost no-one offers advice on *how* to let go of the various attachments that are hurting us. We are constantly told that letting go helps us on a spiritual journey, but no-one ever provides directions or points out the landmarks. Surely, if letting go needed no instruction than none of us would be in the predicament where we attach to harmful thoughts. Yet we all are, at least to some degree.

This chapter aims to rectify this lack of instruction and knowledge. In particular, this chapter will provide a run-down of the philosophies behind the mantra of 'letting go'. We will briefly cover Buddhism and how letting go relates to attachment and other Buddhist principles. Next, we will explore the topic of letting go in more detail; what it actually means to let go and how we can teach ourselves to let go of harmful aspects of our everyday lives. To summarize, this chapter deals with *what* letting go actually means and *why* you should let go.

In the following chapters, we will deal with topics such as *how* to let go as well as the actions and perspectives we need to embrace in our lives to rid ourselves or unhelpful desires.

## Historical Context, Traditions and Other Philosophies

Let us begin with Buddhism. Buddhism is a major world religion, with approximately 350 million followers around the world. Buddhism originated around Northern India and Nepal approximately between 600 and 400 BCE. Buddhism follows and reflects on the teachings of a man known as the Buddha, a philosopher and sage who travelled and taught various ideas and concepts. The Buddha aimed to tackle the problem of suffering in the world; his teachings are often referred to as an antidote or cure for suffering or the 'unsatisfactoriness' of life.

The Buddha conceptualized life as being inherently imperfect. Even if we are not directly in pain, our lives are never complete. We never seem to be able to achieve fulfillment, happiness and contentment no matter what circumstances we live in. The Buddha himself was originally a prince of his region with all the material wealth and pleasures that he could ever desire. Yet he was not content.

The Buddha left his position as a prince and spent many years wandering, meditating and searching for spiritual answers. Eventually, the Buddha is said to have reached enlightenment (a complex concept that will be simplified for the purposes of this book).

With enlightenment the Buddha found the answer to the problem of suffering which he had been tackling for many years; the secret is to *let go of all your attachments*. The Buddha theorized that the true nature of every person is happy and blissful.

However, this nature becomes obscured by our tendency to attach to things; ideas, events, whatever. The Buddha realized that attachment can never lead to happiness and fulfillment; it can only ever disappoint. All we need to be happy is to let go attachments altogether and realized our inner nature, which is already content and blissful.

To elaborate, all of us have attachments which cause us to pain. Most of us desire to be beautiful or handsome, for example. However, to a certain extent, our looks are beyond our control. We may never be tall, or have a bone structure that allows us to be slender. We may not have a masculine or graceful look about our face.

In these circumstances, the attachment to looking good but the inherent impossibility of this attachment is obviously going to cause us problems; we become insecure or envious in our relationships to others, we become unhappy, we may even waste money and risk our health with plastic surgery and other alterations.

Even if we are someone who is currently attractive, an attachment to our own beauty can only ever bring suffering. We are all destined to age; our skin will wrinkle and our muscles will deteriorate, our hair will become grey and we will get liver spots and protruding veins. Even if we are is fortunate enough to be desirable now, if we attach ourselves to looking good, as we grow older our appearances will fade and we will anguish over what we once looked like and what we look like now, or in the future. Even if we age gracefully, we might suffer disease, disfigurement or a whole host of tragedies that can impair our looks.

The point here isn't for us to become pessimistic, to despair or to embrace nihilistic philosophies. The idea is for us to be realistic and reduce the amount of problems in our lives. We cannot control how we look. We cannot prevent aging, and we may always be susceptible to disease or injury.

However, we can prevent ourselves from being discontent and unhappy about how we look, because as most of us know deep inside, how we look isn't important at all. We are just feeding our vanity. If we want to be happy we need to rid ourselves desire to look good. We need to let go.

Let it be clarified that the following argument and perspective on beauty isn't claiming that personal beauty or looks are bad. We do not need to demonize people who look good, or take no care for our appearance. This perspective on beauty is simply claiming that being too engaged with our looks will only cause us pain. If you are handsome or pretty, you are handsome or pretty. If you are not handsome or pretty, you are not handsome or pretty. We don't need to make it anything more or anything less.

The same perspective on beauty and looks can be applied to most of our desires to conclude how they are bad for us. We are attached to the pleasure of eating good food, yet this pleasure is temporary and if we eat too much we become fat and our health suffers. We are attached to the pleasure of sex, yet this pleasure is temporary also and if we focus on sexual conquest too much, we diminish our potential for meaningful relationships (or anguish over our lack of partners). We are attached to wealth and material goods, yet most of us know that a new 60 inch HD TV or that new sports car doesn't actually make us happier.

When we consider these arguments in detail, we begin to realize that letting go is good for us. We can still enjoy good food, sex and even wealth if they happen to arise, but we do not anguish or lament over the fact that we do not have these things when they do not arise. If we are currently attached to sex or money or another harmful desire, we need to learn to let it go.

## Other Important Considerations

With this in mind, we can now begin to learn the skill of *how* to let go. By knowing and understanding the arguments for *why* we should let go, all of us can now try to let go with a greater degree of commitment and passion. However, before we move on, a few other points about attachment and letting go need to be mentioned.

Firstly, this book isn't intended to be a treatise on Buddhism or encourage you to be Buddhist. The concept of letting go of attachment may be Buddhist in its origin, but it does not belong to Buddhism itself. It is perfectly feasible and realistic to accept and understand that letting go of our attachments is beneficial for us, without accepting or endorsing Buddhism or other Buddhist concepts and beliefs. The phrase 'love thy neighbor' may be Christian in origin, but we can love our neighbors without being Christian. Wiccans and Pagans may believe that nature is sacred, but you can hold that belief and still be atheist or agnostic. All of us can appreciate and hold beliefs that seem reasonable or resonate with us, without belonging to the religion or philosophy from where they arose.

And secondly, the concept of letting go applies to most aspects of our lives. The four previous examples offered (beauty, food, sex, wealth) are often cited and parroted in different spiritual philosophies; most of us accept we need to let go of these desires or to some extent already believe we do not attach to these concepts.

Yet the concept of letting go is far more ubiquitous; letting go is often most profound and life changing when applied to seemingly innocent desires. For example, the desire for people to like us or the desire to improve a relationship are both examples of attachments that we may need to let go. We cannot control other people's perceptions or behaviors; it may be impossible for other people to accept or like us.

It may be the case that certain people, even people we love, have personalities or natures that cause suffering and pain to those around them. We can still love these individuals whilst accepting that we may not ever be able to win their approval or have the relationship we want with them. Similarly, even in more mundane circumstances, we may not be able to get a colleague or associate to enjoy our company; we may just not click or be too different.

Holding desires to 'improve' relationships can cause us pain, even though they seem like honest and good desires to feel. The solution is to take to life for what it is; if we have good relationships with others, we have good relationships we them. If our relationship is bad, it is bad. Do not anguish over what is or is not; we should do what we think is right and be at peace with that.

Even the desire to make progress can be harmful. We want to become better in all aspects of our lives; we want to receive that promotion at work, we want to become skilled at playing the guitar, we want to become deeply spiritual and peaceful. Yet all of these desires can just lead to frustration and negativity.

We may never receive that promotion at work and perhaps we just don't have the talent to play the guitar. If we allow ourselves, we can make almost any aspect of our lives a desire and thus a cause for suffering and unhappiness.

On the same vein, it is important to realize that aversion is also an aspect of desire. A feeling of aversion is a type of negative desire; a desire not to do something, or for something not to exist. We might be averse to doing the housework or visiting family that we are not close to. We might be averse to the taste of particular foods or even powerful, uncomfortable emotions such as fear or anxiety.

All of these aversions are just disguised desires. They can be formulated as such; the desire not to do housework, the desire not to see estranged family (and so on). As with other desires and attachments, these aversions also need to be let go. The housework needs to be done, on occasion. We need to keep in touch with family, even if it can be awkward at first. Being averse to feelings of anxiety and fear just prevents us from moving past these emotions. We need to let them be.

The third and final point to make here is that there are desires which can be considered good and healthy. The desire to be happy or to advance ourselves spiritually is a healthy desire to hold. We do not need to rid ourselves of all desires; rather we need not become so attached to a particular *outcome* if this desire does not arise.

## Take Away's

To summarize, we need to learn to let go because desires and attachments because they ultimately cause us to be unhappy and to suffer. We all have the capacity to be happy and content without being dependent on achieving our desires.

This perspective was first expressed by the Buddha long ago; however it can be adopted for the benefit of people who are not Buddhist and many people have chosen to do so. Our desires and attachments include popularized desires, such as sex or wealth, but also subtle desires such as the desire for positive relationships and progress. Aversions are a type negative desire, which also need to be let go. There are however some desires and attachments which can be beneficial, such as the desire to be happy or contribute to others.

# 2

## HOW TO LET GO

*People have a hard time letting go of their suffering. Out of a fear of the unknown, they prefer suffering that is familiar.*

–Thich Nhat Hanh

## Mindset

To learn how to let go involves a multi-faceted approach. In the following chapters we will discuss some of the practical aspects of letting go; this chapter concerns itself with letting go from a more spiritual and philosophical perspective.

In the Buddhist tradition, letting go has been explained like dropping a hot object. Letting go isn't an action we consciously do; we cannot let go of our attachments with a switch of a mental button or through meditation (or whatever means we imagine). Rather, truly letting go is more of an instinct.

It is a deep realization that our attachments and desires are hurting us. If we were to clumsily pick up a scolding hot object, our innate reflexes would cause us to realize the object is hurting us and drop it. Letting go is like realizing we are actually holding on to that scolding painful attachment; we can then drop that attachment without a second thought.

## Experiential Understanding

This realization may be easy to understand conceptually, however actually internalizing this understanding experientially involves much more skill and practice. Eastern philosophies talk about different levels of knowledge and the difference between knowing something intellectually and knowing something on a deeper, spiritual level.

All of us, at some point in our lives have had times where a concept or idea has just 'clicked'. We may have understood the idea, such as an opposing viewpoint or an academic theory, but we couldn't understand the value of the idea.

Then, at some point, perhaps when we were actively thinking about the idea, or perhaps at some random trigger, something in our minds change. We suddenly open up to the idea in a way we previously didn't imagine. Perhaps we see it in a slightly different light or perhaps it just becomes salient and meaningful in a way it wasn't before. We have a slight epiphany; we begin to understand on a deeper level.

It is this understanding that is required to truly let go. We may often believe that we are not attached to good looks, food, wealth, money, relationships and more but our behavior and actions betray us. It is only through this deeper realization that letting go actually occurs.

This perspective might seem to force us into an unsolvable quandary; we understand that we need to let go of certain aspects of our lives, but we cannot directly force ourselves to let go. However, the solution is to try and make ourselves let go through both direct and indirect methods.

## Methods

Let us talk about the indirect methods first. Although we cannot force ourselves to have deep 'letting go' realizations, we can however cultivate the conditions where these realizations might arise. Think of this like you would for taking preparations to have a good night's sleep.

We cannot psychologically force ourselves to go to sleep. Likewise, nor can we directly control how refreshing and invigorating our sleep is. In fact, directly *trying* to go to sleep almost prevents us from sleeping (it seems to be a recurrent habit amongst insomniacs). If we try too hard to sleep, we just become stressed and anxious, which keeps us awake.

However, we can alter the conditions around us to make sleep more likely to occur. We can make sure that it is quiet and that the room we are trying to sleep in is dark. We can make sure that we have handled all lingering responsibilities so that there is nothing in our mind keeping us awake. We can make sure we are comfortable with pillows and duvets and that we are cool.

It is the same with letting go. We cannot just 'let go' of all our problems and attachments. However, by taking certain actions and preparations (as outlined in the following chapters) we can increase the chances of successfully releasing our attachments.

The other approach is to directly consider letting go. As previously mentioned, you cannot force an epiphany, it just happens. However, by considering the philosophies previously discussed we might cause the knowledge that attaching to certain aspects of our lives is harmful to really sink it.

Owing to this, as we go about our lives, we should learn to consider how our various attachments are harming us. These do not have to be melodramatic, ultra-serious contemplations, but rather small, meaningful realizations.

The next time you eat an extra donut or treat that you didn't really want (or pass up a healthier alternative that was presented) consider how your attachment to the taste of that donut is affecting your weight and your health. The next time you lose your temper, consider how the desire to win an argument or achieve something (or whatever made you angry) is now causing you to suffer. Next time you procrastinate; consider your desire *not* to do work (or a desire to do something else) is preventing you from doing what needs to be done.

When we actually think about it, day-to-day we all

have dozens of little imperfections and faults that are caused by our attachments, which in turn cause us to suffer. We may put on weight, or become frustrated over time or fail to be as productive as we could be. We must learn to see the roots of these difficulties in our attachments; hedonistic pleasures and harmful ideas.

By continually pondering these attachments and monitoring their harmful effects on us, we gradually begin to have a deeper understanding and realization that we need to let go. Then we do.

## Conscious Awareness

This is why the concept of mindfulness and being present is often so emphasized in eastern philosophies. If we are to observe our tendencies and our habits to gain deeper understanding and knowledge of ourselves and the world around us, we need to develop a certain level of concentration and presence to allow us to do so.

If we are not present and constantly practicing our awareness, we simply will never realize how destructive and harmful most of our habits are. If we go about our lives on autopilot, then we don't paying attention when we scoff down that extra donut. We fail to realize the fact that things could have been different. We never get over our attachment to that yummy-donut deliciousness. We put on weight or our blood sugar gets out of control – all because of that donut.

Although the donut example is a somewhat simple and slightly humorous example, it serves as a good reminder for how we need to be present at all times. It is only through observing our desires and our following behaviors that we recognize how these longings lead to negative outcomes. As we realize these desires ultimately bring us harm, we no longer engage with these feelings; we no longer wish to have them. Then we might let go.

It is similar to how a child, growing up no longer becomes obsessed with the toys he or she previously enjoyed. At one time, the child would play with the toys for hours every day. However, as one grows up, the toys begin to seem childish and redundant. The desire to play with the toys diminishes and fades. The child moves on. So should we.

## Mindfulness

Mindfulness also serves another spiritual role that is important when talking about letting go. It is the realization that contentment and happiness is in the here and now. As mentioned in previous chapters, the

Buddha believed our true nature is already blissful and happy. We just need to realize it; which involves remaining in the present.

By observing our sensations and feelings as we go about our lives, we realize the genuine joy of just existing. Owing to the fact that simply *being* is enough to make us happy, we let go of our desires because we no longer need them. We don't look to donuts for happiness – or whatever other external stimuli it may be, we look to ourselves.


## Case Studies

There have been multiple interesting psychological studies on lottery winners. These people won millions of dollars; a dream for many people around the globe. Initially these people experienced an increase in happiness (or to whatever extent psychologists can measure such a nuanced concept such as 'happiness').

However, after a period of around six months, these lottery winners were no longer happier than the rest of us. Their happiness had decreased back to a baseline level as all the complexities and difficulties of life slowly crept back into their lives. They still were not happy with themselves; they still hadn't let go of all the desires and stresses that were causing them to be unhappy in the first place. Winning the lottery didn't help.

## Take Away's

To summarize, although the concept of letting go may be easy to understand conceptually, actually *internalizing* this practice through experience can be much more challenging. The process of letting go is an instinctual process that we cannot force to occur. We can however, through a variety of direct and indirect methods increase the likelihood of letting our desires and attachments go. The predominant direct method is to be mindful of how every day, small attachments and desires negatively impact our lives.

# 3

## HOW TO UNVEIL
## THE BEST IN OURSELVES:
## A NEW MINDSET

*Abundance is a process of letting go; that which is empty can receive.*

–Bryant H. McGill

As previously discussed, we cannot force ourselves to let go of our attachments and desires. However, we can take certain actions to cultivate a peaceful, balanced state of mind where letting go happens naturally. By cultivating certain various attitudes and behaviors, we can employ to help ourselves become peaceful and gentle.

This chapter offers a more holistic approach to developing a different mindset; it presents various topics of contemplation and reflection in a broader sense as another means of helping us on the path to become more balanced and at peace. These topics can be taken as a topic of reflection individually, or simply ideas and concepts that we can reflect on throughout our day.

**Focus on the Present**

Embrace the present for what it is –not attempting to label something as 'good' or 'bad'. Our attempts to convert our present into yesterday will leave us disappointed and discontent. We must accept that the past is gone and there is no way of bringing those moments back.

We need not try to make a moment last forever; everything is impermanent. We need only simply be fully present and embrace every moment, without comparing it to the past or the future. Once we fully embrace the present moment, we will be able to release our attachments to that which is no longer a reality.

Develop the mindset that whatever we have right now is enough – there is no need to compare to something that is not there. We never know what the future has in store, and our plans rarely receive the execution we plan for them.

Therefore, the possibilities are endless – your business may start facing losses, your relationship might come to an end and so on. We can deal with all those things if and when they happen, but until then, why worry about them and ruin the present? Sit back, appreciate what you have and fully embrace it, knowing that it is enough.

Begin practicing the art of living moment-to-moment. Understand that fear is self-created and serves no purpose. Aim for a more meaningful life and begin simply enjoying each and every moment for what it is.

## Embrace Mindfulness

Living in the present may sound simple at first, but putting this idea in to practice can prove much more challenging. One of the first problems that we encounter when attempting to be in the present moment is a lack of concentration. We are so used to worrying about the future, stressing over the past or simply daydreaming, that we are not in the habit of paying attention to what lies directly in front of us. We lack the capacity.

Similarly, to be frank, most of the time our lives are spent doing automated tasks that we do not need to pay attention to. Cooking, cleaning, washing, sweeping, walking, and filing papers (and so on). We all have a tendency to think about other things, especially during the more monotonous periods of our day. It is hard to force ourselves to concentrate and be fully present in aspects of our lives we are not engaged with.

## Mindfulness Meditation

This is why many cultures and philosophies that advocate staying in the present moment also practice mindfulness meditation. Mindfulness meditation is a type of deliberate mental exercise where the practitioner attempts to focus on the here and now (usually by paying attention to the breath).

By taking a certain amount of time every day to focus on the here-and-now, without any distractions or other responsibilities, mindfulness meditation can aid staying in the present moment. Mindfulness meditation also improves our ability to concentrate; by forcing ourselves to be mindful during meditation, we can increase our overall level capacity to be mindful during other times of the day.

The other advantage of mindfulness meditation is overcoming many types of mental hurdles and barriers that may prevent us from being mindful. For example, it is difficult for us to remain mindful whilst we are in pain or experiencing uncomfortable emotions. Our tendency is to flee; to think about something else and distract ourselves.

Alternatively, some of us languish about the pain we are in; we lament the things we could do, if only we were not in pain, or continuously think about how much the pain is causing us to suffer.

Mindfulness meditation helps overcome these damaging obstacles by forcing us to confront experiences like pain or negative emotions. If you are in pain, you sit and feel the pain. If you are anxious, you sit and feel anxious. For emotional states like anxiety, you become intimate with those feelings and just being mindful can cause these states to disappear over time. At the very least they help you live your lives a little more peacefully.

Mindfulness meditation may not make physical states, such as pain, diminish, but they do allow you to come to terms with them. You do not cause torment to yourself because you are in pain; you just allow yourself to be in pain.

Even if you do not want to practice mindfulness meditation, there are a many things we can all use to keep ourselves mindful. One of these is ensuring that we only perform one action at a time. Usually in life, we attempt to multi-task because we find it is more efficient. We talk to others whilst we work. We sing in the shower. We listen to music to clean.

However, such multi-tasking stretches our attention too thin. We cannot fully pay attention to a conversation if we are fully paying attention to our work. Chose one activity to do at a time and give all your effort and attention to that activity. Repeatedly doing this improves concentration and attention to the present moment.

Likewise, even if we do not meditate, we can choose to be mindful during low-effort activities. Walking, listening to classical music or simply watching the clouds go by peacefully in our gardens present good opportunities to be mindful of our current sensations; what we see, what we feel, our emotional states. These activities can supplement or even replace mindfulness meditation.

**Identify Harmful Thought Patterns**

One of the many reasons we attach to certain phenomena and fail to let go of others is due to harmful thought patters, such as negative or critical thinking. This is especially true for adverse thoughts. We may think we could be happy, if only we didn't interact with a certain person. We may be attached to binging on junk food to help us overcome the negativity in our own minds. Learning to develop the attitude of the impartial witness is important in conditioning ourselves to let go.

However, for those of us who have a tendency for critical, negative thought patterns, embracing an open mind can indeed be challenging. For people with depressive or anxious tendencies, mindfulness is a powerful tool to overcome harmful thought patters.

To prevent ourselves from falling in to harmful thought cycles, we need to actually *be aware* of the thoughts we are engaging with in the first place. We then need to recognize how these thoughts are damaging and ultimately the source of our suffering.

**Consider Relationships with Others**

We must be comfortable with ourselves before we can fully even begin to release our attachments to relationships and other people. If we associate our sense of worth to another person or thing, then it will be extremely difficult to let go of that person. We must believe in our personal self-worth before we can truly let go of people.

By harboring a sense of value independent of others, we can better share mutual experiences with other people. In this way, we will be able to relate to people without completely depending on them in order to feel better about ourselves. Spend periods of time alone. Dwell in your interests, watch movies, paint, listen to music or do whatever makes you feel happy and fuller.

# 4

## EMBRACING LIFE FULLY: FURTHER METHODS OF RELEASE

*Breathe. Let go. And remind yourself that this very moment is the only one you know you have for sure.*

—Oprah Winfrey

There are a multitude of methods which we can employ to better help us on the path to letting go and develop a clear, content state of mind.

## Change What is In Your Power

One of the first and foremost things to embrace on the path to a more fulfilling life is to be able to recognize harmful emotions, such as anger, frustration, jealousy etc., when they arise. These may include things which are in our power to change, and some which are not. If we are able to identify what we can and cannot change, we will be able to better handle the various situations life presents.

After we have made it clear what we can change, simply take action and change that which is in our power to do so. The things which we cannot change are things we must make peace with and accept.

## Dealing with Frustration and Other Harmful Emotions

A powerful tool in developing our sense of acceptance is by not engaging with the negative emotion – the frustration, the anger – when circumstances that we simply do not have the ability to change do arise. There is no doubt that many things in life will present things to which our internal self is resistant to.

People may be rude to us; we may get stuck in traffic and experience a little road-rage. We may try and do something that we simply cannot do, even after several dozen attempts. Life is full of events and circumstances that will inevitably 'cause' us frustration.

We must make a conscious effort not to identify and become consumed with whatever emotion we are experiencing. A lot of us, when frustrated or angry, attempt to justify our emotions. We say to ourselves that it is okay to be angry when someone is rude to us; we are in the 'right'.

We may even dwell on petty acts of revenge or fantasies where we stand up for ourselves and give the person who was rude to us a karmic smack-down. When we cannot do something, some of us hit our fists against walls or linger on the thought 'If only I could just do it'.

All of these behaviors are damaging to us. They

prevent us from actually dealing with the emotion of anger or frustration and re-direct those energies into violent and destructive thoughts and actions.

The solution is simply to be mindful of your anger and frustration. Observe the feeling of frustration within, and simply witness, accept and fully feel it. Do not label the sensation as positive or negative – simply observe it impartially. Watch the sensation rise, fall, and eventually pass. Just experience it.

## Monitor Thought Patterns

Similarly, as previously touched upon, another way to help be present and fully embrace whatever life presents is to consistently monitor our thought pattern. We need to be able to filter these thoughts.

It is helpful to take a step back to analyze to what we feel resistance towards – to what we are attributing our harmful emotions as being the source of. *What people, circumstances do we feel aversion for? What are we labeling as the source of our stress or anxiety?*

Having a non-judgmental attitude and adopting an open mindset will have a powerful impact in helping us lead healthier and more fulfilling lives.

## Accept Imperfections

We all want to be better. Most of you are probably reading this book to better yourselves somehow. We want to be funnier, happier, and more intelligent. We become frustrated or feel awkward when we make a joke and no-one laughs or we feel embarrassed when we pronounce words wrong or comically misunderstand their meaning. We look towards spirituality to deal with these feelings of awkwardness or embarrassment as well as to improve ourselves, so we can be funnier and more intelligent and so on.

The true solution is for us to realize our 'imperfections' exist only due to our attachments. We are attached to the notion that we have a good sense of humor, so it is painful for us when we can't make people laugh. We like to stroke our ego with the idea that we are intelligent, so when life demonstrates the limits of our intellect, we feel dumb.

Accept that there is no imperative to be intelligent, funny or all these other characteristics, which in deficit, are taken to be imperfections. Sometimes other people find us funny, sometimes they do not. Sometimes we are blisteringly sharp and sometime we struggle to remember our own names.

The point here is to accept what you are and the traits that you have. Happiness isn't the product of polishing and perfecting your traits in order to be the perfect being. Happiness arises when we accept ourselves and world around us just for what it is.

## Finding Closure

Some people form strong emotional bonds more easily than others, while others are able to let go of their feelings with greater ease. Either way, when we share a part of 'ourselves' with a person we tend to find it difficult to let go of these emotions.

Writing a letter may be useful in such situations. Address the letter to your former partner and let them know how much they mean to you. Share your thoughts about the time you spent together. Even if you do not choose to send the letter, this will help clarify the feelings and emotions that have built up inside.

This helps in accepting our present reality. Having all of our thoughts in front of us on paper can also help raise our level self-awareness. It provides us a glimpse into our thought process. Seeing the words written down and in a proper sequence can help us realize that it is time to let these feelings go and embrace the present, and all of its possibilities which are to come.

## A Shift in Perspective

Putting ourselves in the offender's shoes can help us see from the others point of view, but more importantly helps us realize how we ourselves would like to be treated had we been in such a situation ourselves. This can help us relate to the other person's state of mind, and thus make more logical and stable decisions.

Additionally, having compassion will help dissolve anger and resolves bitterness more easily than anything. Practicing patience and non-anger is key.

The next time you feel anger or irritation towards someone or something they said, remind yourself not to take the offence so seriously. We often become more offended than necessary, and the emotions and feelings of anger are always more damaging to our mental and physical health.

**Gratitude**

Another technique in developing a healthier mindset is to continually recognize that which we are grateful for.

Being mindful of those who are less fortunate than us is crucial to developing a balanced perspective on our own problems. Many of us live in developed western societies and even though at times, our lives may be hard, we rarely faced with genuine adversity. We have food, water, shelter and a whole host of luxuries and creature comforts. We are not forced to go to war or suffer the effects of an unstable and non-democratic political regime.

Whilst we cause ourselves to suffer and fret over that presentation at work next Monday or the fact that we embarrassed ourselves in front of a certain colleague, it can be useful to remind ourselves that there are many other people who are in much more critical conditions then ourselves. Many people are starving or suffering from disease.

It should be noted, however, that the point is not for the suffering and anguish of other people to make us feel better. Rather, it is to help us recognize that most of our problems are rather small and more manageable than we commonly perceive.

By nature we are focused and obsessed with our own lives. We fret and consider all our actions as if we were the focal point of the entire world. When the greatest difficulty we face in our lives is getting people to like us, or dealing with a difficult workplace, we often become consumed and allow ourselves to become completely overwhelmed by these small issues and lose sight of the greater picture.

The result is that even small imperfections and flaws seem magnified to be larger and more significant than they actually are. By reminding ourselves of the struggles and difficulties other people face, we can remind ourselves about our own capacity to deal with our own problems. If we simply take a moment to consider the burdens of someone else, we can develop a more realistic perspective of our own problems.

Additionally, actively reflecting on what we are grateful for – perhaps by writing down these things in a list – can be a useful exercise to help remind ourselves for that which we appreciate in our current circumstances.

## Consider Improving to Benefit Others

Finally, there is even a strain of thought encouraged by some philosophers and gurus that we need to improve ourselves for the sake of other people. We all have the capacity not to just improve our own lives, but to improve the wellbeing and happiness of the people around us.

By considering the trials of other people, we can find the motivation to improve ourselves, if not for our sake, than for the sake of other people. Otherwise all that potential we have to improve the lives of other people on the planet may be wasted.

# 5

## DAILY PRACTICES, STRATEGIES AND TECHNIQUES

*Letting go. Everyone talks about it like it's the easiest thing. Unfurl your fingers one by one until your hand is open.*

—Gayle Forman

Though the ultimate goal is to let go of all our troublesome desires and issues that cause us unhappiness, it is sometimes necessary to take baby-steps.

This chapter suggests various techniques we can employ on a day-to-day basis. We can also embrace the concept of mindfulness and letting go of attachments through many practical ways and may find it useful to employ short-term strategies that can have a quick, immediate impact on our lives.

## Learn a New Skill

Learning a new skill is a fantastic way to practice mindfulness. In our lives we tend to repeat the same actions over and over again. Our brains are wonderful biological machines that eventually form neural pathways that make repeated activities easier and require less conscious effort.

When we first learn to read as young children, we have to actively concentrate on the sounds of each of the letters in the words. Through a great deal of practice, we eventually learn to read most text with little or no conscious effort. None of us have to pay any effort to reading 'stop' on a signpost or the numbers in the yellow pages.

The result is that we fail to be mindful of these basic, everyday activities that we become so acquainted with. Learning a new skill or taking up a new hobby helps bring our concentration and focus back to the present moment; we have to focus on the position of our fingers when we learn to play the guitar or the grammar of our computer code when we learn to program. Learning is an exercise in mindfulness.

Try a new sport - something that will help release some of the frustration we might feel. Some good examples of these are kick boxing, taekwondo, water sports and athletics. Try learning a new language or learn a new dance routine – something you have always been interested but have been scared to take action with. Try cooking a new cuisine - surprise yourself with your abilities.

## Yoga and Meditation

Additionally, many forms of meditation and yoga will help us on the path to feelings of release and relaxation.

Although yoga is more commonly practiced as more of a physical exercise in the West, traditionally one of the main benefits and focuses of yoga was to focus on the breath as a way to become more present. Through the movement of our bodies through the various postures (*asanas*), our mind is given constant practice to continually remain present in every movement and breath.

Meditation practices can vary in style, technique and specific object of focus, however something all practices have in common is the aim to develop a calmer, clearer mind through various concentration, focus and breathing techniques. Some of the various meditation styles include *Shamata* practice (concentration and focus practice), analytical meditation (reflective, introspection type practice) as well as active or dynamic meditation (meditation in physical motion). Investigate the various methods and find one (or multiple) methods which best suit you.

## Animals: Acceptance, Simplicity and Unconditional Love

Spending time with animals – be that in a form of having a pet or simply spending time with sentient beings other than humans - is a great way to help us remain present. Animals naturally have a much greater ability to remain present and accept what already is without judgment, comparison or the need to analyze.

With a pet, one can more easily feel and express emotions. We need not worry about hurting our pet's feelings or about getting unsolicited advice. Pets are also a great source of companionship; they love and accept us just the way we are. Through the company of animals, we may find that we are able to practice the art of loving unconditionally.

Spending time in the company of animals can also be a useful tool for helping us deal with emotions such as stress or anxiety. Animals have long been used to treat depression, as they offer unconditional love and attention. This can be helpful to those dealing with misplaced emotions, loneliness and depression.

Studies have shown that pets can help reduce tension and overall improve our mood and the way we think. Depression and unplaced emotions can leave us feel isolated or lonely. During such times, having a companion in the form of a pet can be extremely beneficial.

Animals are also useful for developing compassion and teaching us how to be gentle. We rarely treat animals with the same derision and disgust we direct against ourselves, and on occasion, other people. When feeling hurt or angry, a useful technique we can employ to bring ourselves back to calmness and gentleness is to think of all the love and affection we feel towards pets and other animals.

Furthermore, animals are also great companions to remind us to appreciate the simplicity of life. Most of the relationships involving other people are often more emotionally complex and consuming. Spending time with animals in the form of a pet is a great tool in helping us remain present.

## Release Emotion Physically

At times, we may simply feel completely overwhelmed with emotion. We may feel as if there are some things that we cannot let go of, memories or stimuli in the environment which we feel have simply consumed us. If we feel the need to express this build up of emotion, simply release it. It will not only make us feel better, but will also help clear out minds.

We are human after all, and it is always good to express our emotions. This way our feelings are released into the open and those around us are better able to understand what we are experiencing. Expressions of release such as crying can be healthy outlets in ways to release buildup resistance and stress our bodies due to stress our bodies and minds have been carrying.

Suppressing emotions can also lead to outburst in the form of anger or frustration, which is also not healthy either. It is always better to express your anger consciously and calmly, rather than keep it bottled up inside. Specific techniques and methods to effectively manage stronger emotions, such as anger and frustration, shall be discussed in further depth in the following chapter.

## Acceptance is not Apathy

A common misconception we often make when trying to let go is thinking we need to accept every part of our lives as they are and become apathetic. We are told that we must be mindful of our feelings and sensations as they pass and arise.

For negatives experiences, such as pain and anxiety, we are told to simply delve into these emotions and become one with them. We are told that happiness is within ourselves and not due to external factors. The overall undertone is that we only need to change ourselves and not the world around us.

This undertone is not what is meant by these spiritual lessons. You can and should make efforts to minimize situations and events that lead to harmful outcomes. Likewise, you can embrace and partake in activities that lead to beneficial outcomes.

Part of the purpose of mindfulness is to examine cause and effect; then influence them to produce better circumstances for yourself and other people. Owing to this, if people, events or activities cause us suffering and negativity, cut them out. It is not all just about our thoughts.

## Consider the Environment: Is it Conducive to Developing a Healthy Mind?

*Do you feel your surroundings are influencing your emotions and thought patterns in a harmful way?* If so, it may be useful to consider a change in your daily environment. For example, trying another job or volunteering in a place which generally makes us feel happy. Animal farms, petting zoos and community centers are some possibilities. Recognize that if it is not immediately possible to alter your present environment, then at least take a step towards what you think your ideal (work) environment would be.

## Train the Psyche

Compartmentalization is a useful strategy to manage the thoughts that we think may be negatively affecting our wellbeing. It can take a little practice to master this technique, but it is really quite simple.

First, mentally visualize a box or folder in your head. Then, whenever you start to dwell on things of the past or start to create stress about the future, mentally 'shelve' these thoughts into this box and store it away on shelf.

## Exercise = Therapy

Exercise in any way is a release, whether it's mental or physical. Try taking an hour each day for an exercise routine of your choosing. Go for a run or try some yoga. Even watering plants or gardening can help reduce stress and increase endorphins. Exercise therapy can be a great tool to aid in one's overall improvement of state of mind.

## Spend Time in Nature

Putting aside some time every week to spend in a natural environment is a fantastic way for us to balance ourselves. Firstly, most of us are not used to spending a great deal of time in a non-urban, non-civilized setting. By removing ourselves from what is familiar, we give ourselves another opportunity to practice mindfulness.

Whenever we go to a forest, an empty field, a stranded beach or cliff, we can direct our attention to the rare and novel sensations around us; the sound of the wind, strong and unbroken over the landscape, a chorus of birds, each with a slightly different pitch and timbre. Really focus on each feeling and impression you experience. Fully take in the beauty of the sunlight as it filters through the canopy, producing a kaleidoscope of shadow and light amongst the leaves.

The second advantage of spending time in nature is to give ourselves another place to think. We are conditioned by habit to think the same thought patterns and produce the same feelings from our trappings. The sight of the refrigerator may cause that sense of guilt from overeating; the sight of the living room might burden us with the need to do some housework.

Going somewhere without these negative associations helps us to realize our calmer more peaceful nature. Furthermore, we tend to associate nature with peacefulness and relaxation. Basking in the uplifting vibes we feel from the landscape and from plants and animals can help us to better manage the other taxing aspects of our lives.

## Art = Release

Expressing ones emotions through a specific outlet can be helpful, especially through a creative outlet. *Why not try recording your thoughts through by writing them down in a journal or blogging?* Methods such as blogging can be a useful tool to share and relate to other fellow human begins. Many people would likely be interested in hearing about your experience and would probably be able to relate and reassure you that you are not alone in your journey.

Painting is also another great way to express our thoughts; it could be a challenge as well as a creative outlet. Our paintings serve as visual reminders of the fact that we have expressed our feelings, and with blogs one can actively track the journey towards a more fulfilled life.

As with many of the previous tips, art is also a great opportunity to be mindful and focus on the present. When painting, make an effort to genuinely engage with the activity; feel the stroke of your pencil or paintbrush against the canvas, relish in the different textures and colors you create.

## Simplify and Create Space

Physically clearing space – be it through organizing and de-cluttering - can also help us discover more mental clarity and see things in a fresh thought perspective as well. It can be useful to take down pictures of a former friend or partner or things we know we are emotionally attached to. Box up the gifts and mementos and take them to the local charity shop.

De-cluttering in this physical sense will serve as another reminder that we have also released the burden and attachment to this person on a mental level as well. Every step should be recognized as another step towards accepting that this relationship belongs firmly in the past.

Visual reminders can also be effective tools in helping us keep a centered, balanced state of mind. Reading and listening to lifting texts and songs can help us move on more effectively. Having an uplifting quote on the wall can also be useful.

Have your favorite quote hung up on the wall, somewhere where you will see it often. If you don't have one, it can be useful to remember messages such as "Loving myself means letting go". It doesn't matter what we have to let go. Reflecting on such messages serve as useful reminders to simply accept and have compassion for what already is.

# 6

## MANAGING OVERWHELMING EMOTIONS

*Let go. Why do you cling to pain? There is nothing you can do about the wrongs of yesterday. It is not yours to judge. Why hold on to the very thing which keeps you from hope and love?*

–Leo Buscaglia

In this section, we shall explore various techniques which can be used when we become so completely consumed and overwhelmed by a particular emotion. We shall first discuss the importance of understanding the origin of this emotion, as well as identify practical techniques to help deal with these emotions most effectively.

## Diffusing Anger Effectively

Before we can let go of an emotion, we must fully understand where it came from, what caused it and how to get release it in an appropriate way. Reflect on what made you angry – *was it a specific person, or situation?* This may help diffuse the hostility and bring a healthy state of mind to express whatever you want to this person.

It's normally not only frustration we feel towards our life and the surroundings, sometimes it can be misplaced anger as well. If we stifle our feelings, our emotions are likely to release themselves through the form of an angry, emotion-driven outburst.

Although it can indeed be difficult, the most

important thing to bear in mind when experiencing a harmful emotion is not to identify with it. For most of us, when we are angry, we willingly abandon rationality. Deep down, we know that most of the time our anger is not warranted and ultimately not very helpful to the situation. Yet, in spite of this, we still allow ourselves to become consumed be the harmful thought. We ruminate and we brood. We plot and we fantasize. We daydream.

A more mindful approach is to remain objective and impartial to whatever emotion we are experiencing. If someone in our lives has frustrated us, we need to take a moment to logically and objectively consider the situation. Perhaps they did not intentionally mean to frustrate us, or perhaps we may have angered them or given them reason to act aggressively towards us. It may be the case that we are both having a bad day and just interpreting harmless words or actions as hostile. By being able to remain objective and not identify with our emotions, there is often an easy and practical solution to most problems.

## Self-Compassion

A simple, but effective way we can teach ourselves to be kinder, it to treat ourselves as if we were children. When a child is struggling with a situation, or in this example, struggling to control their temper, it is bad parenting to scold them, belittle them or to encourage their anger.

Instead, a wise parent offers support, encouragement and logic. A parent would calmly ask their child why they are feeling angry, and then gently guide their child to a solution. We need to learn to do this with our own minds; treat ourselves with the gentleness we usually only reserve for children.

This act of kindness towards ourselves plays a key role in our inner state of peace and well-being.

## Communication is Key

Our emotional outbursts can create barriers between us and people who truly care about us. Having emotional outburst can cause people to view us as an angry person and increase hostility towards one another.

This is why communicating our feelings is so important. Bearing in mind that we cannot control how the offender reacts, it is best to approach these situations with level-headedness and remain objective so that logical, rational communication can be made.

## Focus on the Issue

Many times when we are angry we tend to focus on
other peoples mistakes and get caught up with how
the situation could have been better if the person had
done things this or that way. This essentially acts as an
attempt to not make ourselves responsible in any way.

Contrary, if we are able to recognize that we
ourselves could have reacted in a way more conducive
to finding a solution and have the ability to change
the situation we tend to feel empowered. We become
more self-aware of our mistakes and are confident
that the next time around we will be able to handle
the situation or our emotions in a better way.

## Exercise

In the cases where our emotion has already consumed
our being and rational thought process is no longer
possible, it can be useful to employ physical practices
as a way to aid in emotional release. For example,
practice literally 'throwing' away your anger.

Try going to a tennis court and have a friendly
match with the tennis ball machine. Hitting the balls
can give us a rush which will help release the pressure
and anger built up inside in a more manageable way.
Alternatively, if the hitting doesn't work try throwing

something like a basketball on a wall or small tennis balls in a lake. Be sure to clean up after yourself.

Using a stress ball can also be a helpful tool to alleviate anger and express tension physically as well as vocally. Making faces and expressions will relieve the tense muscles of the face and can help improve mood as the blood flows around the muscles. Associating negative thoughts with something unpleasant has been a technique used by psychologists for a long time.

Normally we are accustomed to thinking that whenever our mind obsesses over negative thoughts, we automatically associate the thought process with the unpleasant thing. For example, wear a rubber band on your wrist, and when you start to go over all the negative things that have happened, start gently flicking it. This will condition you to associate something unpleasant with your negative thoughts.

Ultimately, we need to continually remind ourselves that when we become bothered by something, we can either remove ourselves from the situation, change it or accept it. Holding on to these harmful thoughts or emotions will  simply be more damaging  to us and those around us in the long run.

# 7

## BECOMING A NEW PERSON

*You've got to be willing to lose everything to gain yourself.*

—Iyanla Vanzant

## Self-Growth

The past makes us who we are today. It shapes us, it teaches us, but most importantly the past should always be the past - never to be taken as the present or the future. By identifying the experiences that have taught us, we will be able to feel a sense of closure and perhaps even achievement. This contributes to our self-growth, which is very important.

No one should remain static, exactly the same person day after day. Past relationships play a huge role in who we are and help shape us. Attachments form when a person identifies with another person. This is illustrated when someone expresses their emotions towards another person in a very intimate way; to leave this person and what you share with them behind is very challenging for many people.

As humans we are constantly growing and evolving. We must define ourselves with our strengths, choices, capabilities, thoughts and skills rather than relationships or possessions. Once we begin to adopt this mindset, we begin to program our minds to release our attachments.

We have the power within ourselves to create our own destiny and have an amazing life full of all the happiness this world has to offer. Each of us holds the ability to remain centered, stable and self-fulfilling in all our relationships and aspects of our lives.

Adopting this mindset simply requires daily practice, determination and constant awareness. Once we truly become at peace with ourselves - our thoughts and our abilities - it will be easier to embrace the things that are meaningful in life and to let go of the things that don't matter.

# CONCLUSION

*I demolish my bridges behind me... then there is no choice but to move forward.*

— Fridtjof Nansen

We all want to feel on top of the world, completely happy and content with our lives and relationships. In our pursuit of happiness, we develop aversion to people, places and circumstances which we attribute to be the source of our suffering. We fail to realize that the source of our stress, anxiety or other uncomfortable emotion is self-inflicted.

We attach our happiness to things, circumstances and people and develop attachment to these external stimuli. We also fear when we feel that we may lose any of those desires which we have attributed to being the source of our happiness. Therefore, any type of change or alteration relating to that attachment leaves us in grief.

We let our feelings define us. And that doesn't remain true for only positive feelings. If we are 'used to' the feeling of pain, disappointment, regret or any other negatives emotion, we will most likely find it 'safe' to remain in this state. In fact, such people are most likely to find comfort in their lives and situations when they are suffering.

The teachings discussed here have illustrated that when we cease trying to control the surroundings and the world around us, we open the doorway to innercontentedness and peace. This is why it is extremely important that we let go - because letting go means allowing ourselves to truly experience what is happening and accept it.

That being said, letting go of an attachment is not easy. It requires change in the way we feel about our experiences. It is a slow and gradual process requiring consistent practice.

We have all been hurt in some way or another; there has been something or someone who reminds us of some sort of inadequacy we have or something we were not able to achieve. In most circumstances, this person is ourselves; our own mind constantly reminding us of our failures, causing us to worry about the future. Our mind pushes us to develop harmful desires and attachments, which ultimately cause us to suffer and harm our wellbeing.

However, this does not have to be the case. This book has provided you with the philosophies and knowledge you need to start on your journey of letting go. By having read this book, you should understand the principles of why having desires and attachments are harmful to your own wellbeing. You should be familiar with the process of letting go and the importance of cultivating mindfulness as well as peaceful, balanced states of mind which allow you to dissolve your problems.

You have what it takes to fully embrace life and let go of the self-created frustrations. You are now equipped to handle some of the many complicated situations with a clear, calm mind and make conscious and reliable decisions.

This will not only allow you to feel more comfortable in your skin, but will also make you a happier person. Most importantly, you know have the ability to let go of unbeneficial thoughts and move on with a renewed sense of living.

# SHARE YOUR EXPERIENCE

*This is love: to fly toward a secret sky, to cause a hundred veils to fall each moment. First to let go of life.Finally, to take a step without feet.*

–Rumi

Finally, if you enjoyed this book and would like to share your experience with others then I would like to ask if you for a favor:

**Would be kind enough to leave a review for this book on Amazon?**

We all have the capacity not to just improve our own lives, but to improve the wellbeing and happiness of the people around us. Helping others embrace the present, let go of attachments and live a more meaningful life is a seed we can all share.

You can access the review page at amazon.com by searching 'Letting Go Brittany Hallison' in the Kindle store.

Thank you and best wishes.

# EXCERPT

## MINDFULNESS FOR BEGINNERS:
Relieve Stress, Live Worry-Free and Cure Anxiety with Mindfulness Meditation

We attach our happiness to things, circumstances and people and develop attachment to these external stimuli. We also fear when we feel that we may lose any of those desires which we have attributed to being the source of our happiness. Therefore, any type of change or alteration relating to that attachment leaves us in grief.

Mindfulness meditation is a distinctive type of meditation that focuses on awareness. The roots of mindfulness meditation are to be found in ancient Buddhist practices, who believe that maintaining awareness of the present moment at all times is key to achieving enlightenment.

According to Buddhist schools of thought, through the power of constant and disciplined awareness, individuals begin to understand how phenomena arise, how they pass and how all things are connected. These realizations in turn help people turn away from their attachments, overcome ignore delusion and fruitless desires. Ultimately, for Buddhists, there is no enlightenment without awareness.

Religious and philosophical undertones aside, the advantages of mindfulness meditation remain numerous. It is not only a fantastic concentration exercise, but the healing effects of mindfulness meditation on stress and anxieties are well-documented.

Although several types of meditation are being explored scientifically, mindfulness meditation is increasingly recognized as especially effective. It is the predominant meditation prescribed by health services as a treatment for stress, stress-related disorders as well as anxiety and depression.

Whereas many styles of meditation and new-age practices are rife with pseudo-science and subjective personal interpretations, mindfulness meditation is one style of meditation that you can trust from a scientific standpoint.

In this book, you will first learn about the underlying philosophies and ideas behind mindfulness meditation. You will learn about why it is beneficial to be mindful and why numerous religions and philosophies have embraced mindfulness as a way of life. In the next chapter you will learn about to actually practice mindfulness meditation by focusing on your breath and associated breathing techniques. In the third and final chapter, you will also learn about the practical aspects of meditation, such as how to meditate comfortably for long periods of time as well as how to manage your time to ensure you meditate every day.

From these teachings, you will become intimate with the basics of mindfulness meditation and ready to start discovering the inner peace that already exists within your mind.

## Excerpt from Chapter 2: A Mindful Way of Being

In some perspectives, mindfulness meditation is sometimes viewed as a way of life that one embraces, rather than just the physical practice of meditation once per day. If mindfulness is the cure to wayward thought, which can be responsible for a lot of the stress, depression and anxiety in society, then this mindfulness needs to be constant.

It is of limited use to simply be mindful only when we meditate – this will not help us in circumstances where we are not meditating. Instead, we need to learn to gradually bring the attention and mindfulness we cultivate during meditation in to everything that we do.

Whether we are doing something pleasurable, something unpleasant or something neutral and inherently uninteresting we need to remain mindful nonetheless. We are all guilty of going into autopilot mode sometimes, especially for activities that we do not like or activities that we find uninteresting.

Yet all the activities and duties make up a large portion of our lives – the cleaning and household chores, the work we do not want to do, the favors we perform for others, washing ourselves and brushing our teeth every day and so on. Simply ignoring these actions and not paying attention to them not only gives opportunity for unhelpful thoughts to arise, but it is also allowing ourselves to let the majority of our life pass by, unaware.

## Mindfulness: A Constant Practice

So for everything you do, *do it mindfully*. When you clean, feel the sensations of cleaning; the scent of the soap, the motion of your limbs, the feeling of water on your skin. Ensure that you clean to the best of your ability – getting all the nooks and crannies. When you eat, feel the texture of the foods in your mouth, be aware of the pace and feeling of your jaw as you chew and the flavor of the food. For everything you do, be intimate and engaged with the activity – mindfulness meditation aside, this is bound to make your life feeling more rewarding and fulfilling.

This mindfulness goes for both the positive experience and the negative experiences. By nature we tend to crave pleasurable things – the best food, sex, clean and aesthetic surroundings, etc. However, life by its nature is full of pleasurable and unpleasant things. Trying constantly to avoid all the negative unpleasant sensations is a battle that we will never win – sometimes we will simply be doing something or feeling a sensation that we do not want to feel.

Just like in the section about pain, being averse and resisting these sensations actually just causes us more torment and difficultly. This doesn't mean we become masochistic – we can avoid unnecessary pain and unpleasantness in our lives.

In fact, by being mindful we can learn to skillfully manage and navigate our lives with more tact and prevent, mitigate or avoid negative circumstances which are unnecessary. Ultimately, we do not relish in the pain and unpleasantness we experience in our lives, but rather we simply witness and accept the sensation as it occurs.

# OTHER WORKS BY B. L. HALLISON

Mindfulness Meditation to Relieve Stress, Cure Anxiety and Live in the Present Moment

Meditation for Beginners: How to Meditate to Relieve Stress, Anxiety and Depression and Live Peacefully

The Complete Guide to YOGA: Yoga for Beginners, Yoga for Weight Loss, Yoga Poses, Benefits and More

Social Anxiety Cure: Relieve Social Anxiety, Overcome Shyness and Be Confident for Life

A Beginner's to Internet Marketing: 17 Proven Online Marketing Strategies to Make Money Online and Grow Your Online Business

Facebook Marketing: 25 Best Strategies on Using Facebook for Advertising, Business and Making Money Online

Social Media Domination: Social Media Marketing Strategies with Facebook, Twitter, YouTube, Instagram and LinkedIn

Passive Income: Make Money Online and Achieve Financial Freedom – How to Make $500 - $12 K with Only $50

Procrastination Cure: The Ultimate Solution Guide on How to Overcome Procrastination and Develop Practical Time Management Strategies for Life

Interview and Get Any Job You Want: Employment Techniques and How to Answer Toughest Interview Questions

Chronic Fatigue Syndrome Solution: Overcome and Cure Chronic Fatigue Syndrome Using Effective Recovery and Treatment Methods

Hearing Loss Cure: Get Your Hearing Back and Hear Better Than Ever Before

Memory Loss Cure: Prevent Memory Loss and Improve Your Short Term Memory

Alternatively, you can visit B. Hallison's author page at amazon.com/author/brittanyhallison to see more of her other works.

# ABOUT THE AUTHOR

Brittany L. Hallison has loved reading and writing from a very young age. She has always felt that through books, she is able to make a stronger sense of connection with others - be it with characters, writers or the information itself.

Brittany writes about a wide range of topics including personal growth and development, spirituality and holistic health and wellness. More recently, she has also expanded her writing to working with other authors and contributing to book topics such as marketing and business.

Brittany strives to write about topics which she feels can contribute to others. Her books always aim to offer a source of inspiration, information and a way to overcome a challenge. Nothing is more rewarding to a writer then being able to help people and actually make a difference in others' lives.

"The pen is indeed mightier than the sword."

Made in the USA
Coppell, TX
14 March 2021